W9-BDM-778

Cranberries

By Inez Snyder

Welcome Books™

SCHOLASTIC INC.

New York Toronto London Auckland Sydney
Mexico City New Delhi Hong Kong Buenos Aires

Contributing Editors: Shira Laskin and Jennifer Silate
Book Design: Erica Clendening

ISBN 0-516-25548-7

12 11 10 9 8 7 6 5 4 3 2   4 5 6 7 8 9/0

Printed in the U.S.A.   61

First Scholastic printing, September 2004

Contents

Cranberries grow on **vines**.

Cranberry vines grow
in **bogs**.

People fill the bogs with
water when it is **harvesttime**.

Farmers wear high **boots** to **harvest** cranberries.

The boots keep farmers from getting too wet.

Farmers use **machines** to pull the cranberries off the vines.

Then, the cranberries **float** on the water.

11

Farmers use pieces of wood to move the cranberries together.

13

Farmers push the cranberries onto a moving **belt**.

The belt moves the cranberries from the bog to a truck.

15

Farmers harvest many cranberries in a day.

People look through the cranberries and take out the bad ones.

The good cranberries will be sold in stores.

19

Cranberries are used to make many foods.

New Words

belt (**belt**) a moving band of rubber used for
    moving objects or for driving machinery
bogs (**bogz**) areas of wet, spongy land
boots (**boots**) shoes with high tops that cover
    part of the leg
float (**floht**) to rest on water
harvest (**hahr**-vuhst) to pick or gather plants
harvesttime (**hahr**-vuhst-time) the season when
    fruits and vegetables become ripe and are
    picked or gathered
machines (muh-**sheenz**) things that are made to
    do work or to help make other things
vines (**vinez**) plants with long stems that grow
    along the ground or climb on trees, fences, or
    other supports

To Find Out More

Books
Cranberries: Fruit of the Bogs
by Diane L. Burns
Lerner Publishing Group

Harvest Year
by Cris Peterson
Boyds Mills Press

Web Site
The Cranberry Lady
http://www.thecranberrylady.com
Learn about cranberries and play fun games on this Web site.

Index

About the Author

Inez Snyder has written several books to help children learn to read. She also enjoys cooking for her family.

Reading Consultants

Kris Flynn, Coordinator, Small School District Literacy, The San Diego County Office of Education

Shelly Forys, Certified Reading Recovery Specialist, W.J. Zahnow Elementary School, Waterloo, IL

Paulette Mansell, Certified Reading Recovery Specialist, and Early Literacy Consultant, TX